It was a DRIP DRIP

Dad came in to call me.

"It's time to eat, Jed," he said.

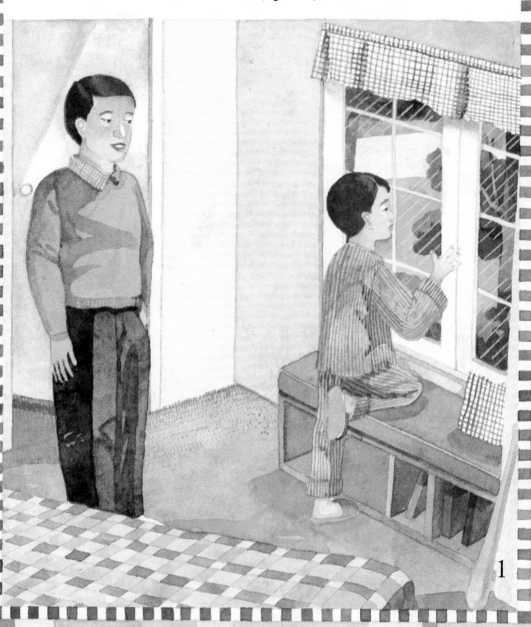

"It's not a day to go out and play," I said.
"It's a DRIP DRIP day."

"I say it's a FISH TRIP day," said Dad.

"A fish trip? Where?" I said.

"You will see," said Dad.

"This is our fish trip," said Dad.
We went in to see the fish.

"So many fish!" I said to Dad.
"And we have to see the jumping fish,"
he said.

So then we went in to see
the jumping fish.

The fish jumped . . .
and jumped . . .
and jumped!

"You said it, Jed!" said Dad.
"It's a DRIP DRIP day!"